Shattering A Façade

ANANYA GOYAL

ISBN 979-8-89233-338-2

Illustrations by

Navya Kasera

To everyone who cry alone
in their rooms

Contents

Broken

It's just a word for some
Just an exaggeration
It's a pity for some
Way to overlook the hurt

But only who have felt it
Will know what is it
I for one know
What it is like to be broken

So just don't say
"It will be okay"
Haven't I tried to be fine
But it's not that uncomplicated

It can never be fixed
It's not a disease cured
It will be a part of you
Forever and more

Because once for you are
You will always be
'Broken Beyond Repair'

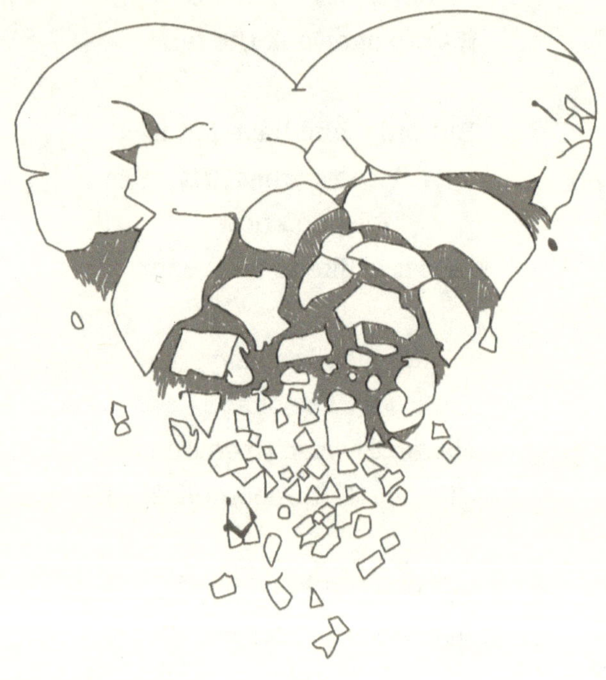

My Worth

The house I built
Went down in an instant
The one with key
Made a million copies

I gave shelter
I became dust
All I have is questions
About my worth

I am an invisible force
With a million faults
The only part seen
Is the one they need

I am stranded and alone
Crumbled all across the floor
No confidence, no fight
Only self-doubt in mind

I try to rise
Not to bleed
Not to be miniscule
Just like my worth

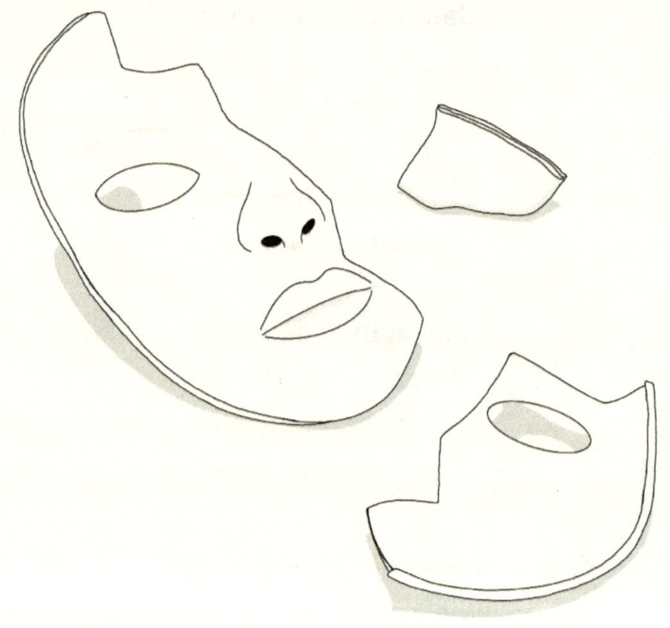

My Feelings True

I am a living corpse
But I can't help
I'm all alone
So you will not care

I want to restart
But the chains of the past hold me back
The scars, rumours and the façade
Why I left behind my smart

I try my best
To love myself
But I fear
It will happen again

I hide my tears and fears
Behind uncountable layers
A smile so fake
Paves the way
Without anything being array

The people I hold most dear
Can't let them see me apart
So I say
"Conceal your tears
Conceal all you can"

But please who is reading this
This should not be true
All I rue
Is not telling my feelings true

No one

My mind is racing
Dark clouds setting in
All I am is scared
No one is getting it

It's a pest
All I do is beg
I am falling
No one is getting it

They say it's an act
They say it's a ruse
It must be true
Cause she agrees too

I am not pretending
I am not victimising
I am not looking to boast
It's me all alone

I lurk in the dark
Death is my vice
A scarf is a hide
No one is getting it

It's just a tightrope
Between the worlds
I am dangling on it
But No one is getting it

The Bridge

There was a bridge so beautiful
Made with love so true
June was its glory
The prettiest one too

Even if it was glass
It was so strong
It made everything pretty
Even when there were thorns

The architects wanted more like this
The one which long lasted
Nothing broke it
Whether it was rain or rocks fallen on its surface

But then I came along
A person who tried to put flowers on it
As soon as I touched it
It cracked like a false promise

I tried to mend it
I tried to glue it
But the more I tried
The more it broke

It was glass
That came crumbling down
It was their dreams
Which I tore

One touch of mine
Broke a bridge of 18 years
All love vanished
And I stood there silent

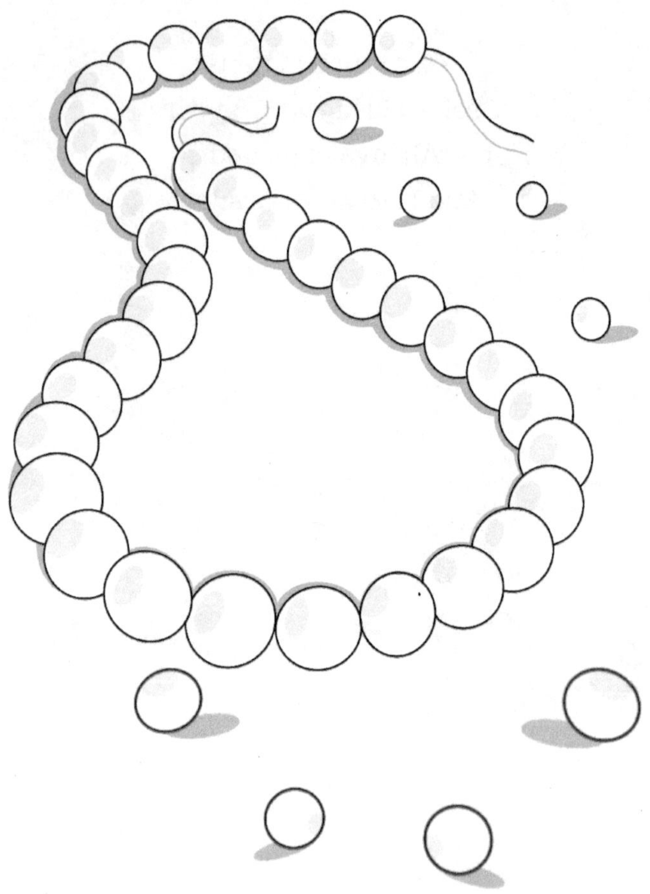

She

The person who I had my trust
Turned out to be a mutt
She stabbed me in the back
Forgetting about our past

She forgot our memories
They were just another day
She left behind our promises
Like a necklace of pearls

She cared for me
She looked out for me
But it was just a game
To pursue fame

Was I a burden?
Didn't she realise I was a person too
I wasn't a doll
Waiting to fall

But when I crashed
I thought for the last time
Wasn't I enough?
For her to be mine

Okay

Okay
Such a funny word
But it has been said enough
Thousands of feelings
Could be yes or a feeling

Okay
A mask to hide
Whatever is deep inside
Keeping a façade
Dancing in the dark

Okay
Something I say
Too many times a day
But deep in my tired eyes
I don't look sane

Okay
Neither dark or light
But it's all grey
Missing the rainbow
But what's a little rain

Escape

I succumbed to my room
Hoping to avoid
The gambler's play
Oh! What a mistake

The walls turned dark
The floor fell apart
There was hole beneath my feet
With a wind so eerie

I fell deep
Into this dark void
Filled with noise
And broken toys

It was nightmare
The of worst all kinds
Not being over
When I opened my eyes

All I need to do
Was find an escape
Something to get me out
Of the haunting maze

I spent hours and hours
Searching for a thing without a name
All I needed was beacon of hope
To help me not fade

I finally found light
So bright and white
An angel to help my plight
Her wings all out
Ready to fly
The wings were spread
I held tight

It was almost over
When I lost all sight
All I could feel
Was numbness in my mind

She had let me go
To lose my mind
It finally dawned upon me

It was no angel
But a devil in disguise
To chain me up
So I couldn't fight

Gems flowing from my eyes
With a rapid burning inside
I let out a scream
All agony waiting to subside

All I wanted was an escape
And not being torn
All I wanted was an out
But there was I on the ground
At the brink of being gone

They say

They say I can
They say it's easy for me
They say it's in my veins
They say stage is my might

They say I shine in light
They say I fly
They say words are my power
They say my voice is a sword

They however don't know
Even in light lurks a shadow
The effort is agonising
Even a bird falls once or more

To stand on stage
Tears me down
Needles all around
Insecurities dancing about

All I am is a girl growing about
I have faults too
Can't be always perfect
Need to break this muse

When a façade this big shatters
I will be free at once
I will have no weight on me
I will be at no one's mercy

Show

The show was set
The stage was up
Glitter all around
Shadows not to be found

Lights all bright
Music all loud
It had begun
The greatest show on Earth

She galloped and jumped
She twirled and swirled
She did all she had to do
In the perfect queue

The crowd cheered
She shone bright
She took the stage
As if it was her vice

The night came to an end
The swarm wanted more
How could she do it
With feet so sore

She withered in agony
But they couldn't know
She was painted red
But why would they care

The Show
Greatest one ever
It came to an end
When she finally fell

My Wish

I don't wish for me
I wish love for everyone
And stars all bright
I wish for light
I wish for truth
I wish for the Earth to renew
I wish for my mum's happiness
I wish my dad luck
I wish my brother peace
For me it is very simple
I wish I wasn't a burden
I wish I was enough

A Day

All my good days
End with tears
Stolen words
And Screams

Why can't I have one day
Where it's all fantastic
Why I can't have a day
Where I'm at my best

Stolen rainbows
Dead unicorns
A smile wide
Is a frown upside down

Happiness as I say
Is a façade
A ruse so real and calm
What lurks behind is what I know

Pain, Agony
An avalanche of emotions
All got ruined by just an action
It was sunshine but now a hurricane

Just a day is what I ask
A day to not rue
A day with no stolen gems
A day so perfect and true

Morning

In my bed all alone
The sun yet to rise
The mirror on the side
Shows how cowardly am I

The birds chirp a melody
All I feel is agony
My scars are all shining
Dried tears on my pillow

The alarm's bout to ring
To wake the person in me
One with a smile so dazzling
And eyes not filled with melancholy

In my safe abode
Under the sheets blue
I lay all tired
Looking at the calm white walls

I try to get up
Sat on the edge
Just a step
I try and take

Feet wobbly, Shoulders aching
A sigh escapes my mouth
Set out to find the zest of life
Is it really as beautiful as they say?

The little kid me
Loved the orange hue
But now I wonder
Is it really so new

Zzz

Sleep

Sleep
A word so familiar
Yet so unknown
Makes me wonder
When will i get my own

I envy those who get it
I envy those who get it good
I envy those whom it loves
I envy those who don't need it as much

Sleep
A mirage so beautiful
I wish I saw it too
Sleep
A land unknown
I hopes I visited too

Sleep
A cloud untouched
Sleep
My one dream

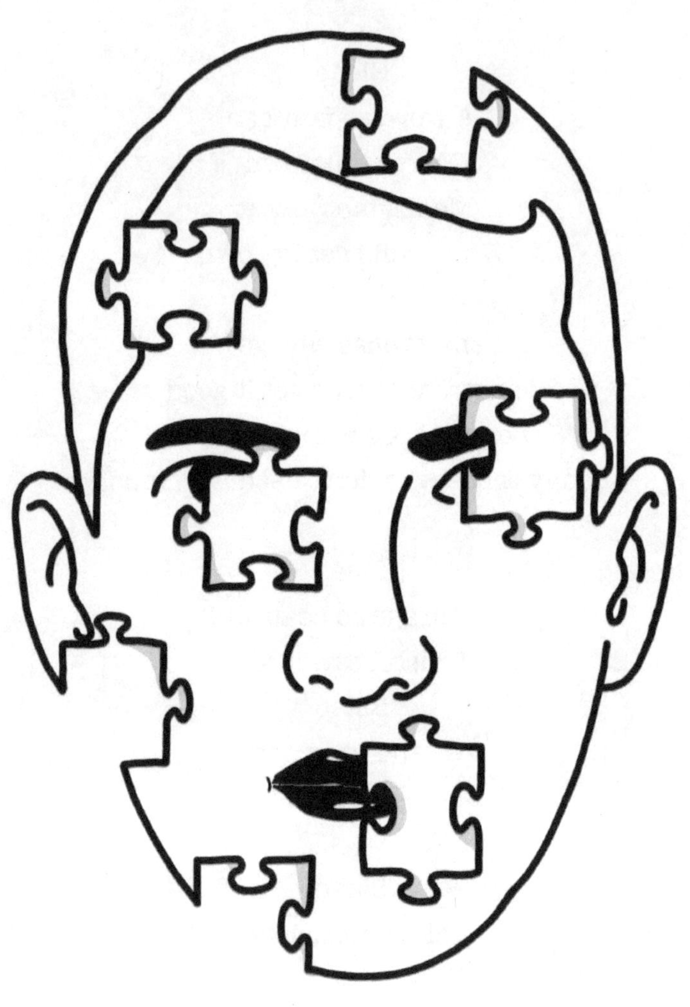

Confused

Confused
I'm so confused
This year is the one that matters
This year decides my life
This is the year of fight

I'm so confused
How they expect it
Choose my life at 17
No alternatives
No roads not taken by

I'm so confused
They tell me to think before I act
But they want a decision so fast
It pains me to not know
My mind fails me this time

I'm so confused
I can't vote
I can't choose my medical care
I'm still a child
But now I choose the course of my life

I'm so confused
This year is the one that matters
This year decides my life
This is the year of fight

No alternatives
No redos
At 17 I decide my life
I'm so confused

Doors

I stood there
Staring at the doors
The toughest on the left
No one had chosen it yet

Everyone chose right
With a bright yellow path
And flowers all around
Beautiful Showers gracing too

The middle door
Yellow path and flowers
Thorns laid out
A bit run down, but not insane

Then there was the one I chose
Yellow paths and thorns
Storms too dark and windy
Still beautiful in a way

My nights were tougher
Their days were brighter
I walked barefoot
I struggled all the way

The first was the longest
The second was complicated
Mine was a different world
However, I was happy
At the end of it all

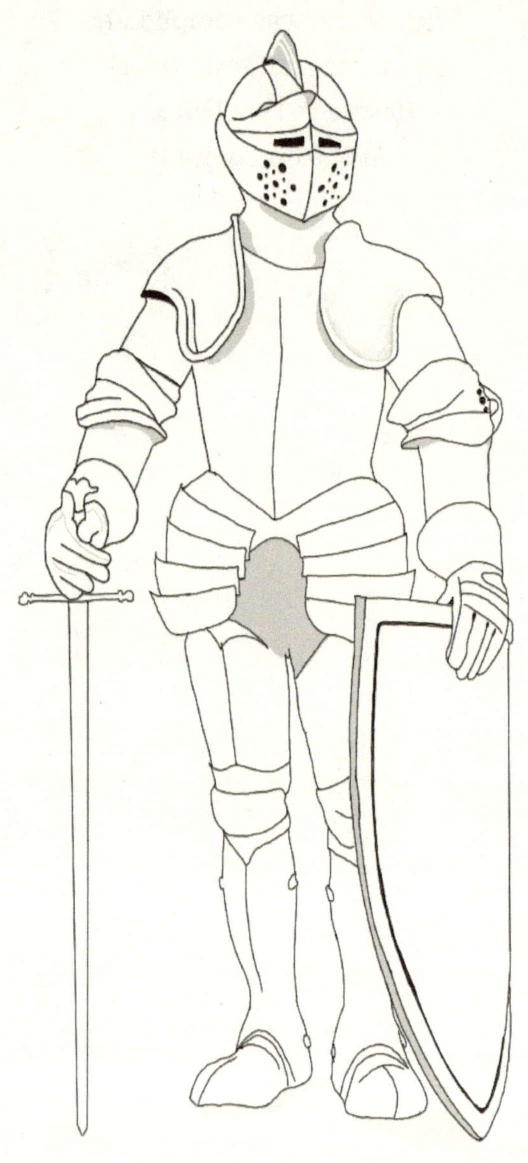

Her

Glass shards on the floor
Blood on my face
Couldn't see her anymore
The devil of the mind

The room was a mess
There was glitter here once before
I tried and tried and tried
But why to fight

The demons, the monsters
All lurking around me
How much more can I tolerate
Let's engulf the pain

All became grey
My vision all blurry
Didn't need a knight
Cause I was mine

The world became still
It was just her and i
This was my chance
Let's end the façade

All I did was stand
All I did was laugh
All I did was embrace
All I did was celebrate

She was I
I was her
We were one
She was my shadow
The one in the mirror
And all she needed was
A little love

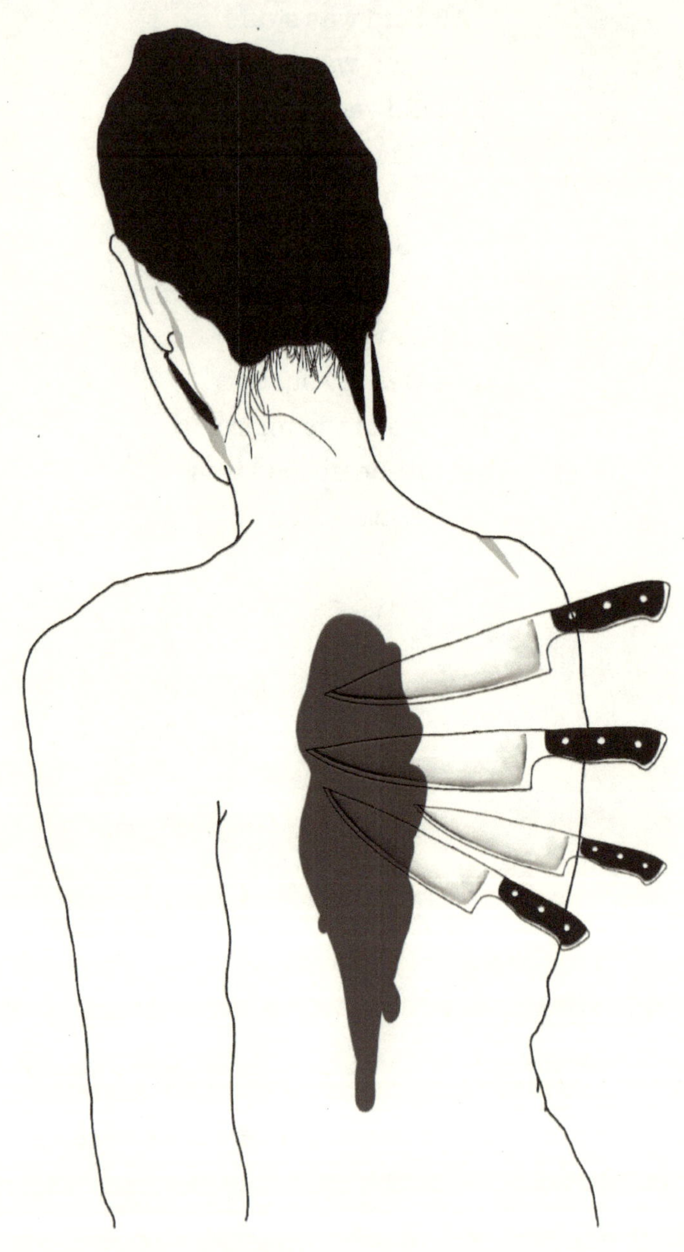

The World

In a crowd
Everyone's on their own
No hands to hold
All alone

Some have a home
Others are lost somewhere
Trying to find their way

With knives in their backs
They walk around
With dead eyes
They search for hope

Too tired I was
The world was broken
The end was near

So I build and build
With magic and fire
Seas and no liars

The world all new
A smile so pure and true
Mended hearts
And no homes askew

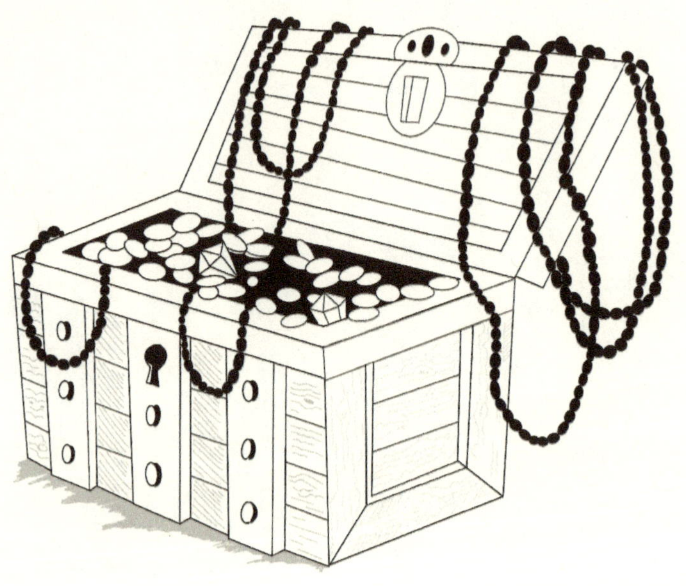

Walls

The moon is up
Like the wall the queen has
Doesn't let anyone through
It hides what she has

The treasure
The gold of her kingdom
The monster lurks outside
Hungry for the attention

It was smart
Pretended as a monk
Injured and helpless
Just needed shelter

The queen
Her heart on her sleeve
Fooled and aloof
Didn't know it was part of a heist

The grand larceny
Nothing left behind
Just a helpless queen
With a mask to hide

Mocked and lost
The queen did fight
Spent hour and hours
And finally she won

Devil sent away
Her kingdom burned down
Fallen pieces of bricks
Glass all around

Seemed impossible to regain
Her strength
Seemed impossible to
Breath again

Let down she was
By her own self
How easily she was fooled
Couldn't even believe

The queen
Smart she was
She built it all up again
From rumbles to a dream

The kingdom with walls all around
Stronger than ever
Yet so delicate

Poison Ivy

Poison ivy
A symphony of beauty. A
Magnificent life growing
Outside. She is what
I aspire to be. A green stalk
With leaves so pretty. No
Ones dares to touch it

Poison Ivy
Wrapped around me. Making me
A bit oblique. Harbouring
My secrets. Making me the
Best I have ever
been. Something which
Protects me.

Poison Ivy
A daunting beauty. Lures them in
And kills in peace. Never scared
Of anything. Misunderstood
It is

Poison Ivy
Such a mystery

A Restart

The sun shone bright
The clouds subside
I ride my bicycle around town
Needing to shout

For once the storm is silent
For once I feel elated
The dragons all slayed
Lives have been saved

I start my journey again and again and again
I'm content to do so
I learn each time a fall
I don't blame anymore

One day I'll reach the end
The so called paradise
But the path is what
Makes it feel so bright

Scars don't fade
But they are my might
Scars with flowers
Giving me new life

After Long Nights

A new flower sprouted
In the garden askew
After long nights of snow
Nature tells a folklore
Spent the night watching
Auroras of neon colours
A new sun rose
A new life tells a tale
From dark to light
The world all decked up and bright
Welcoming the breeze new
Horizon at full glow
The farce ended
After long night of misery
Curtain down
To let in the light

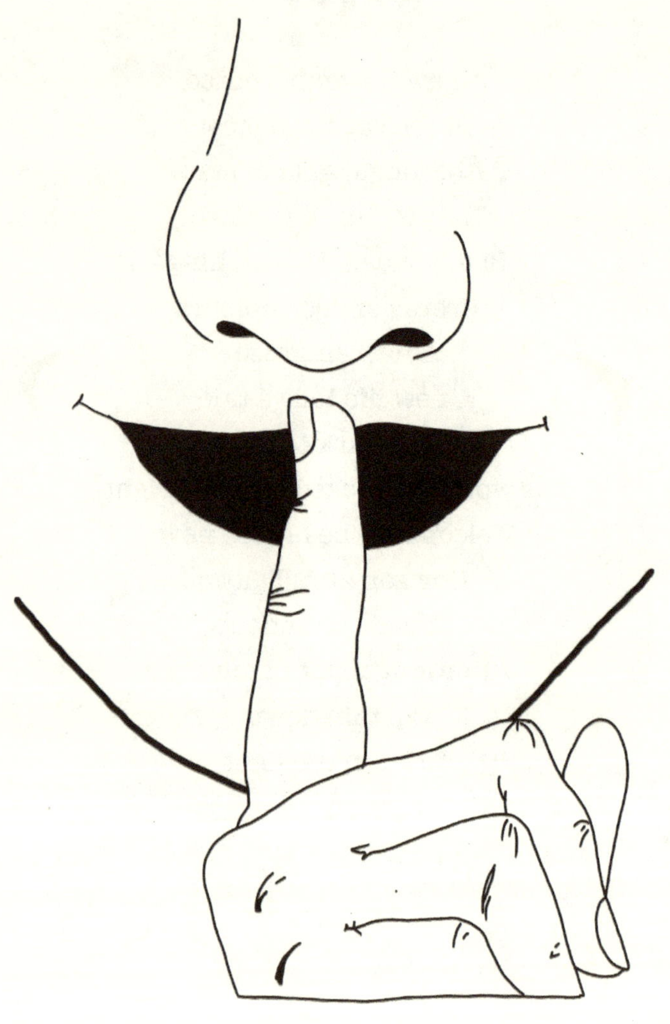

Silence

I sat there
In beautiful Silence
I could hear my heart
I could hear my thoughts

I heard the winds
I heard the kids outside
I heard the AC air
I heard my own voice
Or was it really there?

The serendipity was achieved
The silence was loud
I didn't really know
How come silence was loud?

I sat there
In beautiful silence
I could hear my thoughts
All aligned and clear

Happiness

Hundreds of voices
All in my head
Pure yet so aloof
Patiently waiting to do something
I couldn't do
Nights were brighter
Even storms had glory
Smile on my face
Smile so true and new

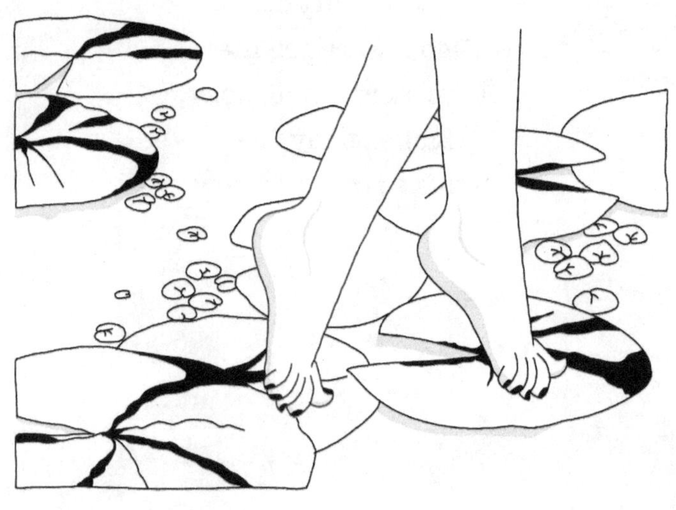

Beauty

This is beauty. The sun all up
and bright. Need no more.
The plethora of green. The wind so
sweet. On the road
I go. Up and away. The path
so unknown. The Lily pads
pave the way. I am true. Not a façade
anymore. Shattering layer by
layer. The ruse was put down. Just me and
my mind. It has stopped now. Not
a blurry confusion. All thoughts contained. The
realisation
finally set in. I can conquer it now.
This is beauty. A clear path. With
music playing. Just me and
my heart. It beats according to
me not the devil
inside. For once I'm not
doubting. Maybe it's the magic
of the valley. Maybe I'm just
me now. Whatever it is
I'm beauty now

Author's Note

The past few years. Infront
Of you. A stranger who
Knows me now. No shadows
Me all bright. Smiles all around

One day you will
Heal. One day you
Will glow. Now the clouds
All dark but one day
The sun will show

Now I take leave. Hope
You resonate with
Me. Thank you
For taking
Part in my evolution
Thank you for being there.

Acknowledgment

To my parents
Who held my hand
To my brother
Who I absolutely adore
To my best friend
Who never judged me
To the people who broke me
Thank you for this opportunity

www.ingramcontent.com/pod-product-compliance
Lightning Source LLC
La Vergne TN
LVHW091121150826
845673LV00002B/928

* 9 7 9 8 8 9 2 3 3 3 3 8 2 *